A Dupatta Is . . .

For Mamas, Nanis, and Dadis, who drape our dupattas and
show us how to wear our culture with pride

A Feiwel and Friends Book

An imprint of Macmillan Publishing Group, LLC

120 Broadway, New York, NY 10271 • mackids.com

Text copyright © 2023 by Marzieh Abbas. Illustrations copyright © 2023 by Anu Chouhan. All rights reserved.

Our books may be purchased in bulk for promotional, educational, or business use. Please contact your local bookseller or the Macmillan
Corporate and Premium Sales Department at (800) 221-7945 ext. 5442 or by email at MacmillanSpecialMarkets@macmillan.com.

Library of Congress Control Number: 2022910004

First edition, 2023

Book design by Mariam Quraishi

Art created with Photoshop CC and Procreate on iPad Pro

Feiwel and Friends logo designed by Filomena Tuosto

Printed in China by RR Donnelley Asia Printing Solutions Ltd., Dongguan City, Guangdong Province

ISBN 978-1-250-82094-5 (hardcover)

1 3 5 7 9 10 8 6 4 2

A Dupatta Is...

Written by **Marzieh Abbas**   Illustrated by **Anu Chouhan**

Feiwel and Friends

A dupatta is fabric
Cotton balls or silkworm cocoons
Plucked and spun into thread
Woven into cloth
Soft and flowy

But a dupatta is so much more . . .

A dupatta is shape
Trimmed into a rectangle
Corners neatly tucked
Edged with lace
Or piped with ribbons

But a dupatta is so much more . . .

A dupatta is color

Dyed to match the deep, rich hues
Of Nani's shalwar kameez

Or the bright, citrus tones
Of my lehenga choli

But a dupatta is so much more . . .

A dupatta is sound

Swooshing, swashing
Like a superhero cape
Flitting, flapping
Like the wings of a bird

But a dupatta is so much more . . .

A dupatta is scent

Cinnamon and cardamom
Peppermint oil and crushed coriander
Sweet, smoky incense lit before sunset
Driving away evil spirits

But a dupatta is so much more . . .

A dupatta is place

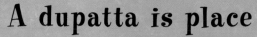

Ajrak from Hala
Chunri from the Cholistan Desert
Phulkari from Bahawalpur
Balochi-tanka from Quetta

Swati embroidery from the Swat Valley
Kashmiri-tanka from Muzaffarabad

But a dupatta is so much more . . .

A dupatta is function

Shielding

Protecting

Sheltering

Veiling

Rocking

Comforting

But a dupatta is so much more . . .

A dupatta is art
Fabric splashed with color
Patchwork, appliqué, embroidery
Beads, lace, sequins
Motifs, block prints, patterns
A masterpiece worked by hand

But a dupatta is so much more . . .

A dupatta is beauty
Silky, sophisticated
Trailing like a robe
Crimson-red for a bride
Draping henna-stained hands

But a dupatta is so much more . . .

A dupatta is fun

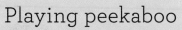
Playing peekaboo

Building cushion forts
with dupatta canopies

Pretending to be Dadi,
wrapped in a sari

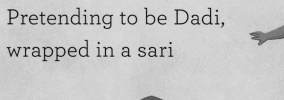

A picnic blanket for a
surprise lunch

A napkin for cleaning
sticky hands

A rope to play
tug-of-war

But a dupatta is so much more . . . .

A dupatta is faith

As Dadi rolls out her prayer mat

Five times a day

An ittar-scented dupatta awaits

Fastening it firmly in place

She raises her hands up in prayer

Allowing her worries to slip away

But a dupatta is so much more . . .

A dupatta is legacy

Handed down through generations

Tucked away for special occasions

Creases smoothed out

Shoulders braced for a powerful speech

But a dupatta is so much more than fabric, shape, color, sound, scent, place, function, art, beauty, fun, faith, and legacy . . .

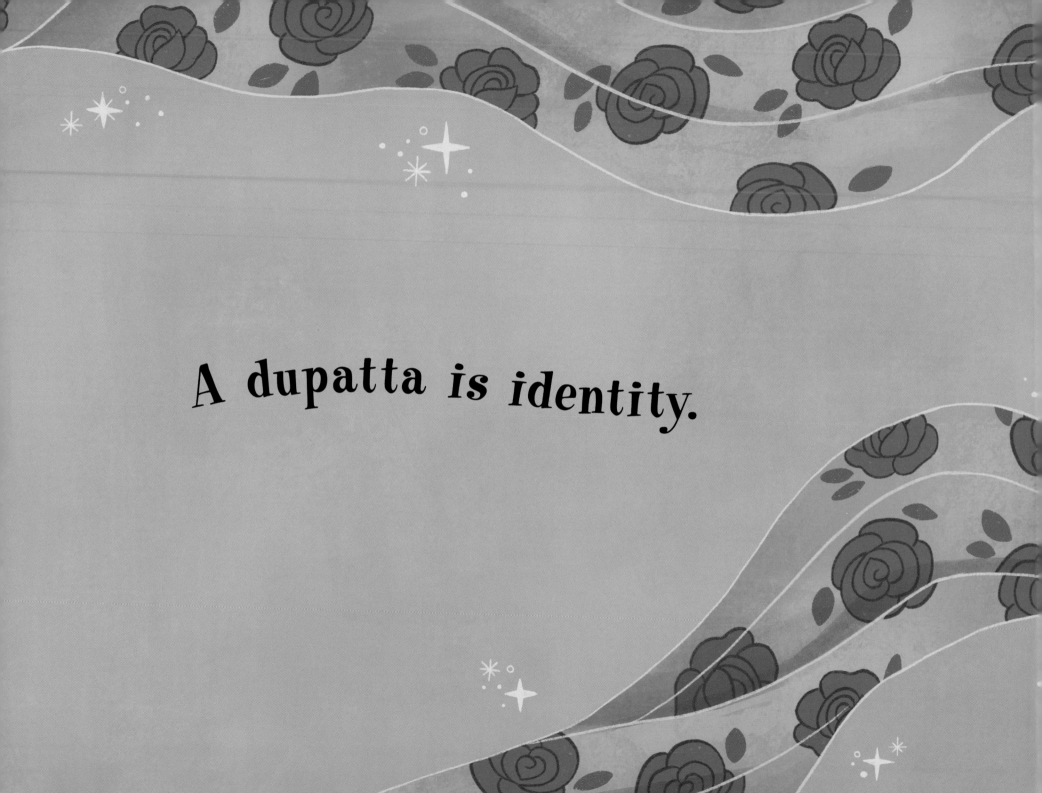

A dupatta *is* identity.

Originally a symbol of modesty, a dupatta is a long, wide scarf traditionally worn as part of the national dress of Pakistan, the shalwar kameez. While that symbolism still continues today, many now wear it as an accessory. It is also worn by people of India, Bangladesh, and Sri Lanka.

The embroidery and fabric styles from which dupattas are crafted often vary depending on where it was made! Locals can often identify where you come from or where you bought the dupatta based on the regions' famous, iconic patterns.

Glossary

Shalwar kameez: a long tunic and a baggy pant, the traditional dress of Pakistan, paired with a dupatta.

Lehenga choli: a fancy crop top with flared pants often worn especially for weddings.

Ittar: an essential oil derived from flowers that is used like a perfume, especially for prayer-time. Muslims pray five times a day on a special mat. Dupattas for prayers are usually white, and a special one is set aside for prayers and rolled into the prayer mat.

Nani: maternal grandma

Dadi: paternal grandma